# LIVING WORDS

Other works by Michel Quoist
also published by Gill and Macmillan
*Prayers of Life*
*The Christian Response*
*Christ is Alive*
*Meet Christ and Live*

MICHEL QUOIST

# LIVING WORDS

Translated by Colette Copeland

Gill and Macmillan

First published 1979 by
Gill and Macmillan Ltd
15/17 Eden Quay
Dublin 1
with associated companies in
London, New York, Delhi, Hong Kong,
Johannesburg, Lagos, Melbourne,
Singapore, Tokyo

Second impression 1979

Originally published in France by
Les Editions Ouvrieres, Paris, under
the title *L'évangile à la télévision*

7171 0988 7

Grateful acknowledgment is made for the inclusion of
extracts from *The Jerusalem Bible,*
© Darton, Longman & Todd Ltd
and Doubleday & Company Inc. 1966, 1967, 1968
which are used by permission of the publishers.

Typeset by Joe Healy Typesetting, Dublin
Printed in Great Britain by Richard Clay (The Chaucer Press) Ltd.
Bungay, Suffolk

# Contents

Foreword

What are you Living for? 1

Who do you think Jesus Christ is? 7

Christmas, or Love has Taken Root on Earth 14

No Prophet is ever Accepted in his own Country 21

Listen to the 'Other', Listen to God 28

Jesus in the Desert or the 'Other Aptitude' 34

The Transfiguration or the 'Other Face' 41

The Samaritan Woman or the 'Other Thirst' 48

The Man Born Blind or the 'Other Look' 55

The Wheat Grain that Fell on the Ground or the
'Other Life' 62

Have you Given Life to your Children? 68

Is the Church Changing? 75

The Doors of Life 81

# Foreword

These sermons were first delivered on television and a great number of viewers asked me to publish them in book form. At first I was reluctant but not, as might be imagined, through any feelings of humility. Like most people who express themselves in one way or another, I am happy when people who tell me that they have been helped by my sermons ask me for the text. But therein lies the problem — these are, precisely, sermons and televised at that. They were written to be heard not read, and I am always afraid that very few people will find in a reading of these sermons what was experienced and understood when listening to them. Furthermore, in the context of the mass of 'The Lord's Day' on television, I was addressing several million viewers from all walks of life and of different cultures, many of whom did not completely share my faith. I made an effort to express myself as simply as possible with the help of concrete images and examples but without detracting from the depth and meaning of my message, so as to reach as many people as possible.

Loftier minds will perhaps confuse simplicity with simpleness. But then, if more modest ones are able to understand me, it doesn't really matter.

These texts, however, should not be taken as 'examples' of homilies. Whilst taking the Gospel as my base, and I hope without straying from it, I have attempted in some of them to answer questions which had been put to me (for instance, on the younger generation, the feast of the Holy Family or changes within the Church, the feast of the Holy Trinity). But there again, there was no question of treating the whole subject—how could I have done that in ten minutes of television time?—but simply of offering a few basic reflections to clarify the subject.

Finally, I sometimes refer to certain topical events which I have not modified here. They are part of my constant efforts to try and root the message of the Gospel in present-day living.

Thus, in spite of all these reservations, I hand these texts over to you. May they at least help a few of you to reach and know Jesus Christ a little better, the living Word of the Father, who I hope can give reason and meaning to all our lives.

# What are you Living for?[1]

The Gospel of Jesus Christ according to
St Matthew — 4:1—11

*Then Jesus was led by the Spirit out into the wilderness to be tempted by the devil. He fasted for forty days and forty nights, after which he was very hungry, and the tempter came and said to him, 'If you are the Son of God, tell these stones to turn into loaves.' But he replied, 'Scripture says: Man does not live by bread alone but on every word that comes from the mouth of God.' The devil then took him to the holy city and made him stand on the parapet of the Temple. 'If you are the Son of God' he said 'throw yourself down; for scripture says: "He will put you in his angels' charge, and they will support you on their hands in case you hurt your foot against a stone."' Jesus said to him, 'Scripture also says: "You must not put the Lord your God to the test."' Next, taking him to a very high mountain, the devil showed him all the kingdoms of the world and their splendour. 'I will give you all these' he said, 'if you fall at my feet and worship me.' Then Jesus replied, 'Be off Satan! For scripture says: "You must worship the Lord your God and serve him alone".' Then the devil left him, and angels appeared and looked after him.*

A man goes to a railway station and asks the booking clerk for 'A railway ticket please!'

'Where to?' inquires the clerk.

1. Homily for the First Sunday of Lent.

1

'I don't know, I just want a ticket!' the man replies.

What would you think of such a request? You would surely think that the man was a bit deranged!

Sometimes we are like that man. I mean, we don't always know where we are going, or the purpose of our lives.

What are you living for? Many would answer that they were living for their children; others would add that they wanted to build a better world. But what world? And what do you want for your children?

For Christians, Lent is a privileged time when we can reconfirm our life's goal and make new choices. Choices which are often painful and demand sacrifices from us.

Jesus too had to make sacrifices. He was a man as other men. He didn't play at being a man; he didn't 'pretend' to be a man. It was gradually, through prayer and meditation, in the presence of his Father, that he began to understand the mission he was meant to carry out. Throughout his life he was dreadfully tempted to impose himself as other men do, through power and might. But God does not impose, he proposes. Because he loves man and he does not violate him. Jesus often needed to repeat to himself, in the silence, in the 'desert', that he was not on earth for his personal benefit, but that he had been sent by his Father for the good of his brothers, to liberate them from their individual and collective alienation and to enable them to acknowledge together, beyond temporal happiness (but without

2

excluding it), an unimaginable dignity, that of the Son of God.

Several of his disciples collected and condensed their own unique and symbolic accounts of Jesus' struggle to remain faithful to his mission — we have just seen an extract from St Matthew — and if we reflect on the three temptations he was faced with, we shall find that they are also ours.

## The temptation of consumption

The first temptation is one I shall call 'the temptation of consumption'; 'If you want, you can change these stones into bread,' — that is, if you want, you can feed all men. They suffer and they hunger, they have no work; you can alleviate their material misery. You can perform miracles, the 'economic miracle'!

'Man shall not live by bread alone', Jesus replies, 'but by every word that proceeds out of the mouth of God.'

Let us understand this well: Jesus is asking us to dissociate ourselves from earthly gains. In his prayer, he teaches us to say: 'Our Father who art in heaven . . . give us this day our daily bread.' We must fight for this daily bread, to say nothing of a pat of butter. We must fight for ourselves, for our brothers, for all mankind. But what he asks of us is that we fight against this alienating consumerism and against the illusory belief that this is where happiness lies. Jesus tells us that our heart needs a different kind of nourishment. Parents, who daily discover the needs of your children, who know how much they need not only material well-being but your time, your atten-

3

tion, your words, your love, you surely understand what I mean.

Like the child, man needs God's love, his Father who has spoken and who has something to say to everyone. As long as men do not hear his word and as long as they do not live by it, they will open their mouths (whether physical or spiritual) wider and consume even more. They can even form a society consecrated to consumer products, but deep down there will always be a gnawing hunger that will turn them into malnourished, anguished people simply because they are starving and they don't know what they are starving for — or rather who they are starving for.

They are poor children who do not know their father; poor children born of an unknown father!

I am sure that you agree, that you are saying: 'It's true, the world is mad! So is society.' But we forget that we are part of this society and that we are participants in this madness. We are *all* slaves of consumerism.

Think of that little god, your car. Think of the comforts of home, your children's toys stacked in a cupboard while they prefer to play with an old shoebox; the books and magazines which will never be read; the masses of records which are getting more expensive all the time and which do not satisfy any more; his innumerable expensive ties, her many silk scarves . . . and so on and so forth.

We hunger for bread. Do we hunger for God?

4

## The temptation of power

The second temptation of Jesus is the temptation of Power, to put his Father's power to personal use. He resists: 'You shall not tempt the Lord your God.' That is, you shall not ask God for favours; you are the one who must serve. The strength of Jesus lies in the fact that he put himself entirely at the disposal and service of his Father and brothers.

We are tempted to use God, to have him on our side (I was going to say 'in our pocket') individually and collectively.

Collectively, through the ages, many human group-ings — nations, races, states, governments, armies and political parties — have tried, and are still trying, to use Christians, the Church, and God to their own ends with slogans such as 'God be with Us', 'Christ-ians be with Us', for Victory, Order, Revolution.

Individually, we often recite the *Our Father* in reverse: 'Our Father who are in heaven, *my* will be done.' We become the centre of things, we usurp God's place. Inevitably, many people then turn away from God because he has not obeyed them.

## The temptation of idolatry

The third temptation is that of idolatry. At this point, you are perhaps saying to yourself: 'This time, it doesn't concern me because it's to do with pagans who worshipped idols in ancient times.'

Alas, the world is full of idols — from that huge idol called Money which we all more or less worship even if we are trying to topple it off the pedestal to which the 'system' has elevated it — to the myriad little idols in front of which we prostrate ourselves daily: our packet of cigarettes or our cream buns; such and such a singer; television; fashion; our bodies or someone else's body. And at a deeper level, we worship our ideas, our ideologies . . . All these little pieces of ourselves which kneel before these stand-in gods cause us gradually, and sometimes unconsciously, to live prostrate, flat on our faces, incapable of getting up and living upright and prostrating ourselves (this time of our own volition) before God.

The Holy Spirit can guide us to the desert too. In the midst of the noise of our actions or in the silence of our hearts, he beckons us.

Even today, because we have come to church, or because we have switched on our television sets, Jesus Christ speaks to us through his Gospel. He asks: "What happiness are you fighting for? What kind of a world are you building? Are you exploiting God, or are you, rather, serving him and your brothers?"

Today, my friends, Jesus Christ is asking us 'What are you living for? What is the purpose of your lives?'

# Who do you think Jesus Christ is?[1]

The Gospel of Jesus Christ according to
St Matthew — 16:13—19

*When Jesus came to the region of Caesarea Philippi
he put this question to his disciples, 'Who do people
say the Son of Man is?' And they said, 'Some say he
is John the Baptist, some Elijah, and others Jeremiah
or one of the prophets.' 'But you,' he said, 'who do
you say I am?' Then Simon Peter spoke up, 'You are
the Christ,' he said 'the Son of the Living God.'
Jesus replied, 'Simon son of Jonah, you are a happy
man! Because it was not flesh and blood that revealed
this to you but my Father in Heaven. So I now say
to you: You are Peter and on this rock I will build
my Church. And the gates of the underworld can
never hold out against it. I will give you the keys of
the kingdom of heaven: whatever you loose on earth
shall be considered loosed in heaven.*

As you can see, opinion polls were not invented
by politicians. Two thousand years ago, Jesus himself
used them. Of course he did not hire the services of
Gallup or Harris — he canvassed his disciples directly:
'Who do people say I am?' he asked them. 'Who do
they think I am?' And they answered, 'Some say you
are John the Baptist; some, Elijah; and others Jeremiah or one of the prophets.' 'And you,' Jesus asked,
'Who do you say I am?' 'Christ, the Son of the Living God,' Peter replied.

1. Homily for the feast of St Peter and St Paul.

People in power always worry about their image, their popularity. Did Christ have any such worries? Not in the least. On the contrary, the Gospel shows us a Christ who always refused the admiration of people who wanted to make him king. He was pre-occupied with the success of his mission — did mankind understand what he had come to accomplish? Had they discovered his true identity? He had joined humanity unobtrusively, incognito, so as not to impose himself through power and might but to reach the weak and the poor.

'Who do you say I am?' Jesus' question still stands, and has stood at the core of history and of man's heart for twenty centuries. And it crops up in thousands of books, conferences, discussions — on radio and television. It is the essential question, fixed in time like an immense invitation to love — no one can escape it.

'Who do you say I am?' The question must be answered. I won't go into the historian's reply, which is too brief and incomplete. I shall also gloss over the answer that Jesus was a great man, a prophet. But I shall dwell on the Christian's answer which operates on two levels: first, that Jesus is the son of God but belongs to the past; and second, that Jesus is the son of God and belongs to the present.

## The mind and the heart

I respect the historian's view because it is a necessary one. But on its own, it can only provide one avenue which leads nowhere. It is impossible to study Jesus in a history book; it is only possible to study him by making him a part of our daily experience, in

8

our personal and communal lives within the Church. Intellectual knowledge is not real knowledge. Would you claim to 'know' your spouse if all the information you had were a passport and some childhood memories as retold by his or her friends? You know your spouse because you live together, because you share your work, your joy and your sadness . . . and most of all because you love each other. 'Only the eyes of the heart really know' says St Exupéry's Little Prince.

Faith is reasonable — but it is not a form of 'proof'. *God invites us* — Jesus said to Peter who had recognised him, 'For flesh and blood have not revealed it to you but my Father in heaven' — God invites us to this faith which is a meeting of love, while at the same time allowing us space for freedom and risk.

## Jesus Christ is more than just a prophet

Today, as 2,000 years ago, many believe that Jesus was a prophet. An extraordinary man who preached and practised the most beautiful message of love that this world has ever known. I often meet people who believe that Christ was a prophet and I say to them:

'Draw life from this message and you will build yourselves; stalwart and united with others of good faith, you will build a world of justice and peace. And if you are honest and receptive, you will perhaps discover a mysterious force at the core of your lives and your actions for your fellow human beings. And at the centre of this force, an infinite love will beckon you. Then you will perhaps see the shape of a face emerge and you will know that it is he — the Lord, Son of the Living God.'

## Jesus Christ — man of the past or man of the present?

Finally there are the Christians. No more intelligent or better than others but who, in the wake of Peter and countless disciples throughout history, recognise and have absolute faith in Jesus. This is what Christian faith is all about. It is not merely a belief in God (millions of people believe in God without being Christians), but a firm belief in Jesus of Nazareth. It is the decision freely taken that this man was neither a clown nor a liar or madman. It is discovering in him someone more than a prophet, someone who came to reveal God to us by showing himself: 'He who sees me sees the Father', someone who came to liberate us individually and collectively, who died and was resurrected so that we could be renewed in a new world. This is where the two levels of faith, which I mentioned earlier, come in: belief in Jesus as a man of the past, or belief in Jesus as a man of the present.

When in an assembly of Christians I ask: 'According to you, where was Jesus Christ resurrected to?' inevitably there is a long embarrassed silence. Then someone finally speaks up: 'To the sky', signalling upwards with a movement of the head.

To the sky? What does that mean? Up there in the clouds? Well, no. Jesus resurrected lives among us, not in a physical sense of course as 2,000 years ago in Palestine but nevertheless in an absolutely real sense. He foretold it:

'Know that I am with you always; yes to the end of time.'

'Where two or three meet in my name I shall be there with them.'

'If anyone loves me he will keep my word, and my Father will love him and we shall come to him and make our home with him.'

'I tell you solemnly, in so far as you did this to

one of the least of these brothers of mine, you did it to me.'

This is the major demarcation line between Christians who believe in a past-tense Christ resurrected 'up to the sky' in the sense of having left this earth, and those who believe in Christ, present tense, resurrected but living today among us.

The first group tends to rely completely on a concept of religion that unites man to God who is 'in heaven' and 'in the past'. They faithfully follow all religious ceremonies, which to them are commemorations of past events: the birth of Christ at Christmas, the main points in his life, and his death on Good Friday. They will pray, their eyes lifted to heaven, to ask him *above* for forgiveness for those *down below* who walk in 'this vale of tears' while awaiting entry into their 'real home', the Kingdom of Heaven. The more virtuous ones try to imitate the life of Christ, their Brother and Model, who is no longer among them.

The second group also adore their 'Father who is in Heaven' but it is in this world, and with the same faith, that they search for Jesus, dead and resurrected, living today among them, inviting them to join him, 'incarnating' themselves too and uniting with him (and not just by imitating him), to work with him in the reign of the Father who is 'already among us' as Christ said. They do not celebrate the 'memory' of Christ but his mystery unfolding itself daily in the history of man, the mystery of which they are a part, with and in his Church.

*Jesus Christ among men? That's hardly fitting!*
The idea of a God living among mankind complicates everything! One can well understand why

many people would be tempted (excuse the pun) to send him back to where he came from, in the same way as you would deal with that inevitable person in your neighbourhood who is forever knocking at your door asking for a favour, or your signature on a petition, or your membership in an association, to whom you politely show the door . . . and close it on him to preserve your peace.

To admit that God came as a man among us is itself very difficult. But in the eyes of many good people, it's certainly not fitting that he apparently did not wish to 'cling to his equality with God', as St Paul tells us, 'but emptied himself to assume the condition of a slave'. It is for this reason that a lot of good souls 'defend' God and fight . . . to have him reinstated. They can turn a blind eye to that 'folly' of 33 years, but that in his excessive love for man-kind, he should be obstinate to the point of 'living among them', of *identifying* with prisoners, the starving, the homeless, and all poor people . . . to the extent that one can't go out of doors without bumping into him, is just too much. One can't go to work, to school, shopping, a union meeting or even a political rally! . . . without having him under one's nose and hearing his perpetual murmur, 'Whatever you do to the least of my followers, it is to me that you do it!' All this becomes unbearable because it changes everything in the Christian heart. And yet, this is what true faith is!

My friends, Jesus Christ is asking us, 'Who do you think I am?'

Would that we could humbly reply: 'O Jesus, I admit secretly that I would have preferred you to have been a prophet, I would have preferred you to

12

have abandoned Earth for Heaven. It would be so much easier.

'But I believe with all my strength that you are the Son of the living God.

'I believe with all my strength that you are among us spreading your infinite mystery.

'Thus I who want to be your disciple come towards you to meet you and to try and work with you and all my brothers of good will so as to save man and to save the world!'

# Christmas, or Love
# has Taken Root on Earth[1]

Beginning of the Gospel of Jesus Christ according to
St John — 1:1—18

*In the beginning was the Word: and the Word was
with God and the Word was God. He was with God
in the beginning. Through him all things came to be,
not one thing had its being but through him. All that
came to be had life in him and that life was the light
of men, a light that shines in the dark, a light that dark-
ness could not overpower.*

*A man came, sent by God. His name was John.
He came as a witness, as a witness to speak for the
light, so that everyone might believe through him.
He was not the light, only a witness to speak for the
light.*

*The Word was the true light that enlightens all men;
and he was coming into the world. He was in the
world that had its being through him, and the world
did not know him. He came to his own domain and
his own people did not accept him. But to all who did
accept him he gave power to become children of God,
to all who believe in the name of him who was born
not out of human stock or urge of the flesh or will
of man but of God himself. The Word was made
flesh, he lived among us, and we saw his glory, the
glory that is his as the only Son of the Father, full of
grace and truth.*

*John appears as his witness. He proclaims: 'This*

1. Homily for Christmas Day.

*is the one of whom I said: He who comes after me
ranks before me because he existed before me.'*

*Indeed from his fullness we have, all of us, re-
ceived — yes graces in return for grace, since, though
the Law was given through Moses, grace and truth
have come through Jesus Christ. No one has ever
seen God; it is the only Son, who is nearest to the
Father's heart, who has made him known.*


Two thousand years ago on this night, Caesar
Augustus Emperor of Rome ruled 'the whole earth' —
so goes the Gospel. Have you heard of Caesar Augustus?

Today, as every year, the whole world has stopped,
not because of Emperor Augustus but because of a
baby born 2,000 years ago whose name was Jesus.

It's Christmas!

Christmas today has changed — it's become commer-
cialised and pagan. Everyone agrees on that. It's
become a time of excessive eating and spending; a
time to trap sentimental people into overspending
on gifts, trimming pine trees and breaking open the
bubbly. But I won't dwell on this, not because I
ignore these deviations and perversions but because I
know that when thick smoke rises and catches in
your throat and brings tears to your eyes it's because
a fire has been lit.

*Come with me to see the fire*

This fire is an irresistible leap of love which today
is felt in every heart and is expressed (however clums-
ily sometimes) through gift offerings — a doll, a train
set, a glittering array of clothes, chocolates and
mince pies.

It is that feeling of forgiving affection which inspires us to invite Aunt Matilda over even though we are no longer on speaking terms because of her gossiping. And it makes us invite old Grandpa too even though he's going to bore everyone by repeating his story about Christmas in the trenches for the hundredth time.

It is that burst of affection which even crosses prison walls where things are a bit better on this special day and the arms on that particular battlefield are laid down for a few hours.

But it's short-lived, some of you will say. True, but name one other birthday that can inspire so much love on earth every year. Others will insist that people don't know what they're celebrating. That's true too but does the fire in the hearth burn less because we don't know the hand that lit it?

My friends, since the coming of Jesus a fire has been burning on earth.

What exactly is this fire whose Christmas flame is a sign of his mysterious presence in the heart of man?

*He is the burning fire on earth*

As with everyone else, my teens were a time of searching for some sort of meaning to my life. What was the purpose of living?

I remember stopping in front of a bookshop window, fascinated by the cover of a book on display. The title was spread over it in large letters, I WANT TO SEE GOD. And I said to myself, 'If he exists, I want to see him too, to know him, to talk to him. But where do I find him?' Later I was to find out that the child whose birth we are celebrating today, told his friends, 'No one has ever seen God!' But he also added that 'Whoever sees me sees the Father,' and 'No

16

one reaches the Father except through me.' Then I understood that you could only meet God in Jesus Christ. But was I to continue my search? Who was God? Was he simply the Source, what the philosophers call the First Cause?

I learned from St John that God 'is' love. *Love itself.* And that is why when he came on earth, he did not appear as an almighty master, but in a stable, a little naked baby, his only riches being an infinite love. This realisation came to me like a shock: God was love and Jesus was love incarnate.

My friends, it is he, the fire burning on earth. That's what Christmas is.

*Love does not constrain, it liberates*

But why must this happy occasion be tinged with sadness? Alas, it is also a time when we are more aware of the suffering in the world. It's because the stronger the warmth is, the crueller the cold seems. Two-thirds of the world's population suffer from hunger; millions of people have no jobs, no homes, no freedom. The amount of arms and weapons capable of destroying the world grows and grows.

What is this love that causes so much suffering?

'It's not love, it's the lack of it.'

'Then let God give it to us!'

But love can't be imposed, it can only offer itself. Where would love be if it said 'I want you to love me, I'll force you to love me!' Man's terrible greatness lies in that he is free to refuse God's love, to refuse to love his brothers as God has asked him. And God can't force us because love is not constraining, it's liberating.

I don't want to be a puppet on a string manipulated by a God who would programme my life, leaving no room for risk.

17

I don't want a God who would build a just world in place of man.

I don't want a God who would prevent me from doing evil whilst allowing me to do good.

I want to be free to choose whether I want to punch someone on the nose or shake his hand, because without that freedom I would never know if, when I offer my hand, I'm offering my friendship.

I want to be free, not through arrogance but because I want to love and be loved.

*Love is a battle*

And so, the fire of life is burning on earth but the earth isn't catching fire. Has love clashed with man's liberty and thus failed? Was Jesus wrong in not being a dictator, in coming to us with empty hands and leaving in the same manner to return to his Father?

I'll end with two observations.

The first is that Jesus has only just come among us. His arrival, in the context of the history of the world, took place only yesterday. We forget that we are only at the beginning of Christianity and that no fruit can mature unless the seed germinates first.

The second observation is that if Christ has planted the seed then, with him, we must nurture the plant. The victory of love is total in the life of Jesus but ours is the responsibility for forging this love in time.

We must, in the same way as the Virgin Mary a long long time ago, say *yes* to the daily annunciations. All our lives, every new morning, this *yes* waits to be touched by love to make it bloom. Otherwise no man, no institution, no structure or society can hope to be built upright and solid.

Don't think for one moment that this is just an idealist's golden dream and that it's easy to love. Love is a battle, its criterion of authenticity is 'other people'. As Jesus said, 'Love your brother as you would love yourself.' This means simply that we must want for others what we want for ourselves, for example:

— We want to have enough to eat, then we must also want everyone to have enough to eat and work to that end.

— We want work, an honest salary, a home, schools for our children, a dignified and respected old age, then we must want these same good things for all our brothers.

So tell me my friends, do you think it's as easy to fight for others as it is to fight for ourselves alone? And when we're fighting, is it easy to do it for love? No. It's as false to have a so-called love which doesn't need any effort as it is to engage in a battle without experiencing love. In fact, because of the weight of the selfishness and pride which we come up against in ourselves and the world around us, that is, sin, loving means being exposed and vulnerable in our fight for others and being crucified by them.

The child of Christmas didn't escape this tragic battle, but in him and by him, love emerged triumphant!

Yes my friends, since the coming of Jesus, a fire has been burning on earth. A fire that will never die. The naked babe of Christmas opened up another story within the world's story, an epic of love triumphing over selfishness, injustice, pride and hate. An epic of unending, eternal love.

So light your candles, offer your gifts, eat your Christmas pudding and sing! Love has taken root in

19

the world and we believe it with all our strength. It will flower because millions of us believe it, because this love is a person and that person is God . . . Emmanuel, God is with us: Happy Christmas!

# No Prophet is ever Accepted in his own Country [1]

The Gospel of Jesus Christ according to
St Luke — 4:21—30

[At the Temple of Nazareth after the reading from
the Book of Isaiah, Jesus declared . . .]

*'This text is being fulfilled today even as you listen.'
And he won the approval of all, and they were astonished by the gracious words that came from his
lips.*

*They said, 'This is Joseph's son, surely?' But he
replied, 'No doubt you will quote me the saying,
"Physician, heal yourself" and tell me, "We have
heard all that happened in Capernaum, do the same
here in your own countryside".' And he went on, 'I
tell you solemnly, no prophet is ever accepted in his
own country.*

*'There were many widows in Israel, I can assure
you, in Elijah's day, when heaven remained shut for
three years and six months and a great famine raged
throughout the land, but Elijah was not sent to any
of these: he was sent* to a widow at Zarephath, a
Sidonian town. *And in the prophet Elisha's time
there were many lepers in Israel, but none of these
was cured, except the Syrian, Naaman.*

*When they heard this everyone in the synagogue
was enraged. They sprang to their feet and hustled
him out of the town; and they took him up to the*

1. Homily for the Fourth Sunday in Ordinary Time.

*brow of the hill their town was built on, intending to throw him down the cliff, but he slipped through the crowd and walked away.*

Nothing goes right any more . . . The honeymoon is over and they already want to kill him! Yet it had all started so well.

Back in his native country, Jesus returned to the temple of his childhood which he used to attend regularly. But on that day, in his sermon, he made a violent attack. This is the substance of what he said to the faithful:

1. In fact, your interest is to 'profit' from me.
2. Strangers and pagans are more disinterested and thus more open than you. It is to them that I must go.

Well, put yourself in their place. Admittedly it is an infuriating sermon. We would have reacted the same way. Of course, we wouldn't have dragged our parish priest to the top of a tower with the purpose of throwing him down . . . but we certainly react in the same way in a verbal manner: 'These priests today! They've a nerve to criticise us and call us bad Christians, we the faithful of the parish. And the 'good' Christians are naturally those outside the parish who are nothing like us!'

*Self-interested Christians*

First of all, let us examine our conscience. Are we not Christians out of self-interest and habit? We are like the congregation at the temple, we accept the Lord but on the condition that he uses his power for our benefit. In fact, what we want is a God who is an indulgence-bank on which we can draw the cheques we need; we want a God who fulfils the desires we

22

ourselves cannot satisfy; we want a God who can give us a better world without our having to dirty our hands working for it — otherwise 'What good is religion?'

We are making a tragic mistake. God isn't a supermarket for indulgences, or some kind of sugar-daddy or an all-risk insurance policy. He isn't a 'providential' political leader for the foundation of a just society or a genial Minister of Finance for economic miracles. He is first and foremost a loving Father who waits to be loved freely by his sons.

Let us not make any mistakes here, otherwise the Lord will repeat his words to the faithful at the temple that no prophet is well received in his own country, and he'll turn his back on us, leaving us to the indifference of our good conscience and our miles of selfish prayers.

## The 'Habitués of God'

My friends, are we not also very often 'habitués' of God? Now, habit is a scourge which paralyses and ends up snuffing out all life.

You all know some habitues of love, for instance. Perhaps even you yourselves have been frightened to find that one day you have nothing to say to each other, you are bored. And then you think, well, at least we have the children to occupy us, to distract us . . .

It's so terribly sad — habitués of love where love has slowly waned and faded away to nothing.

The same happens with religion — habitué Christians! For many people, God is like an old relative inherited by generation after generation, one that doesn't really cause any problems until the day when we perhaps look a little closer. 'It was at our wedding/

23

when grandmother died/the baptism of our first-born . . . that we noticed. It was a great shock!' we declare.

Or else when we were younger, we were perhaps part of a religious youth movement. And so on.

Little by little, God has become 'Someone'. He came to us in the form of Jesus Christ and we understood that this Christ was not to be found in the grave-yard of history but in life itself where he daily awaits us. So we formed a relationship with him and perhaps we even worked together in the Christian community and the human community generally. And then, it became a case of 'Well you know how it is, the pressures of work, the daily worries . . . we lost touch.' And like two friends who haven't seen each other for a long time, when they eventually see each other in a crowd, they barely recognise each other.

'Habitué' Christians who don't know, or have forgotten their God, are a sad thing.

## To practise or not to practise

I see two attitudes here. There are people who insist on certain religious habits, certain practices and prayers which they want to pass on to their children because they feel their children should be raised the way they themselves were raised. Others, particularly among younger people, find it both ridiculous and hypocritical to go through rituals which, for them, have lost all meaning. And they maintain that one can believe without having to practise a religion.

Both attitudes are wrong. Just as the motions of love *without* the sentiment are a degrading and odious caricature, it is true to say that any practice of religion in a general sense *without* a true encounter with the living Christ is a terrible comedy if not a tragic illusion. What would you think of a couple in love who said 'We are madly in love but we don't talk to each other anymore, we don't kiss and we have separate rooms'?

So what do we do when we have become 'habituès' of God? Drop it and forget all about it? No. Continue the way you are, whatever your ups and downs, your doubts and your trials, because true love is measured by its durability. *But* through all your actions and movements, do all you can to find the living Jesus Christ who is the source as well as the end.

My friends, if our faith, the outward signs of our faith, and our obligations are declining, it is because the face of Jesus Christ is vanishing from our sight.

*Salvation for all*

After the examination of conscience, I said I would propose a short reflection on salvation. Here it is.

At the temple, Jesus clearly affirmed the universality of his mission — to the Jews this was scandalous. But there was worse. Not only did Christ go amongst strangers and pagans, he also gave priority to sinners and poor people. Look at it this way: Jesus took his meals with thieves and smugglers; he conversed with corrupt officials and forgave them; he talked with prostitutes and told these little ladies of the night that they would 'precede us in the Kingdom'. It is to the beggar, the vagrant who might even be a murderer, that he opens the gates of Paradise first.

There's the scandal! It seems that Jesus ignores the religious and moral habits of those he reveals himself to. Why? Because the most important thing is their faith in his person, 'Whoever believes in me will have eternal life.'

But what is even more disturbing because it seems so contradictory, is Jesus at the famous scene of the Last Judgment. You will recall his words: I was hungry, I was thirsty, I was a stranger, sick, in prison, etc. and you helped me or didn't help me. (see Matthew 25:35—44).

Jesus is pointing out that those who were saved as well as those who were condemned didn't know that the person they had accepted or rejected was *himself*. We will therefore be judged solely on the way we have behaved towards our brothers.

For many of you, this is a kind of consolation because it hurts you to see, among your loved ones, those who either don't know Jesus Christ or have ceased to know him. Consequently you can assure yourself that if they truly live for others Jesus will welcome them. He himself said: 'Come, blessed of my Father . . . because I hungered and you gave me food . . .'

## Why must Jesus Christ be made known?

The question poses itself. If, to be saved, it is enough to put ourselves entirely at the service of our brothers, do we need to make Jesus Christ known? Do we benefit more from knowing him?

I myself found the answer following a painful but beautiful episode.[1] I know a woman whose baby had been torn away from her during the war. Later she found out that the baby was alive and had grown up into a young man. After a long search, he was finally located and one day, his mother told me of the scene of the reunion. She was sitting down, overcome with emotion, with her son on his knees before her,

1. Already described in *Christ is Alive*, p. 135, Gill and Macmillan, Dublin 1971.

26

caressing her face with trembling fingers. 'You're my mother, you're my mother,' he repeated. Then suddenly I understood. For twenty years this boy had been the son of this mother. He had everything since she had given him life. Yet he had nothing because he didn't know the source of that life. He didn't know the face of his mother. He didn't know her name. He had no way of returning the love she had given him.

If there were only one man on earth who didn't know Jesus Christ but lived like Christ himself simply because he loved his brothers, everything would have to be done all the same to enable him to encounter and get to know Christ. Because living is beautiful, being saved is beautiful, being loved is beautiful, but it is all tragically incomplete as long as we don't know who to thank for it.

My friends, Jesus Christ gives to all men. But he waits for us to return *everything*, freely, through our actions.

# Listen to the 'Other', Listen to God [1]

The Gospel of Jesus Christ according to
St Luke — 10:38—42

*In the course of their journey he came to a village, and a woman named Martha welcomed him into her house. She had a sister called Mary, who sat down at the Lord's feet and listened to him speaking. Now Martha who was distracted with all the serving said, 'Lord, do you not care that my sister is leaving me to do the serving all by myself? Please tell her to help me.' But the Lord answered: 'Martha, Martha,' he said 'you worry and fret about so many things, and yet few are needed, indeed only one. It is Mary who has chosen the better part; it is not to be taken from her.'*

My friends, Luke the Evangelist has told us a story with which, ladies, I am sure you will identify.

You are in the kitchen preparing a meal. Your guests have arrived and next door in the living-room your husband is serving drinks. He calls to you in the kitchen: 'What will you have, darling?' But darling is up to her elbows in bechamel sauce and hasn't the time.

Your friends, of course, told you not to go to any trouble on their behalf. But all the same, you can't serve them just any old thing. And no one is offering to help. They're just sitting there chattering away and you're getting increasingly annoyed.

1. Homily for the Sixteenth Sunday in Ordinary Time.

Two thousand years ago in Bethany, the guest was Jesus. In describing the visit, Martha's annoyance, Mary's apparent passiveness, and Christ's intervention, what is Luke trying to tell us? Let me quickly say that it has nothing to do with the choice between action and contemplation, the temporal and the spiritual, militant life or life of prayer, as common belief would have it. As if one excluded the other and vice versa! Then what is the story really about?

First, Jesus' reproach to Martha is not about her work but her agitation, and second, he proclaims once more that the priority of priorities is the Word of God.

*We are 'slaves' of our worldly activities*

Jesus says to Martha: 'Martha, Martha, you worry and fret over so little . . ' He hasn't said 'over nothing' because he's hungry and will want to eat shortly. He does not reproach Martha for cooking but for being too preoccupied with it and becoming its slave. This in turn will alienate her from her friends — that is, in her preoccupation with the job, she risks overlooking people.

What about us? We have to nourish ourselves, it's a duty. The Lord doesn't ignore this, he fed the crowds, he prepared meals for his apostles, he told us to daily pray to his Father for our 'daily bread'. You have to work to live and raise a family. But frequently are we not, like Martha, pressured, shoved, submerged, ending up *slaves* of our jobs and other duties?

Ladies, are you not slaves of your houses, of your children's cleanliness etc. Dust here, stains there, your kitchen floor, your living-room draperies; vacuum cleaners, washing-machines, etc. etc.

And you, gentlemen, you have repairs to your car, your wife's iron has been waiting two months to be fixed, your attic needs cleaning out; your tools, your backyard, your garage, and heaven knows what else!

We're swamped! We rush here and there, constantly short of time which we desperately need. And the more we rush around, the more out of breath we are and the less efficient we become. Until the day when a heart-attack or a 'de-pression' stops us in our tracks . . . if not death itself.

And all the while, our fellow humans, our brothers, those who are nearest to us, wife, husband, *children*, neighbours, colleagues at work or in organisations we belong to, all the people around us, wait. We no longer have time for them, We don't have the time to listen; their words don't reach us any more. Monologue has replaced dialogue and we become all the poorer, shut up in our solitude.

'You fret,' said the Lord to Martha. 'You fret,' says the Lord to every one of us, 'while your brothers wait at your door wanting to meet you, to talk to you . . .'

*The spiritually undernourished*

On the other hand, two thousand years ago in Bethany, the Evangelist tells us that 'Mary . . . sat down at the Lord's feet *listening to him talking.'* The Lord himself had said that 'Man does not live by bread alone but on every word that comes from the mouth of God.' To those who told him one day that his family had arrived and was waiting for him, he said: 'My mother and my brothers are those who listen to the word of God and put it into practice.'

Do we listen to this word? We wouldn't want to miss the words of such and such a politician on the radio; we wouldn't want to miss a particular debate on television. That's fine. But are we as avid to listen to the word of God?

Some time back a film was called *The Big Feed*,[1] that revealed our mentality in a most filling way. Whilst we suffer from all kinds of digestive disorders brought on by 'terrestrial overeating', are we not at the same time spiritually undernourished?

*God speaks*

God is not the eternal silence that some people complain he is. He spoke and he speaks. St Paul has told us that after God spoke through the prophets, he spoke through his son Jesus Christ and Jesus Christ broke the silence of mystery for us. He revealed the Father, and proclaimed the Good News through human actions and words. The Evangelists have given us the essence of these actions and words in the little book from which we read a passage on Sundays. Are we familiar with the Gospel, we who declare ourselves Christians — that is to say, *of Christ?*

Have we had the intellectual honesty to read a few serious articles, or even a book, on how to read and meditate on the Scriptures? But at the same time, do we believe enough to go to Church, whether on our own or in a group, to place ourselves before the Word of God, simply, like little children who come to learn and be nourished?

God, like all lovers, desires only one thing — to reveal himself to those he loves. He awaits us with a bouquet of flowers and words of love on his lips. But we don't turn up . . . we're too busy in the

1. A French film entitled 'La Grande Bouffe'.

kitchen, we're anxious . . . and consequently unavailable.

*We have no time to listen to him*
I can hear some of you say: 'We would very much like to bow at the Lord's feet, but we haven't the time.' Is this quite true?

— Perhaps we only have fifteen minutes to read the newspaper. Well, perhaps sometimes it would suffice to just read the headlines.

— We always have ten minutes to spare for a bit of chit chat about the weather with our neighbour next door or our friends. Five minutes would be enough, and they could be used for a warm handshake, a friendly smile and a few words of concern.

— We spend a good couple of hours at a 'highly important' meeting. Surely an hour and a half would be more than enough provided we used the time well, to discuss things in depth and decide on a course of action.

Others will go on to say: 'It's not our fault. We live in crazy times. First you have to fight for better living conditions and then the problem will be sorted out.' Indeed! It's true that you have to fight with all you have, but is that enough?

If we are not careful there will always be a tiny transistor at the bottom of our hearts, permanently powered by long-life batteries and churning out assorted banalities, while foolish figures dance on the screen of our imagination.

If you don't know how to be recollected, even in the midst of your most worldly activities, or when engrossed by your most just and generous actions, you will never hear the Lord's Word ring within you. You may listen to the Word, read it, share it, but it will take root only in fertile ground.

## A holiday for re-creation

My friends, many of you are on your holidays. Some of you have returned. Others haven't gone yet. And yet others will not be going at all. I am thinking particularly of those of you who are sick and those who are too old. Instead of lying on warm sandy beaches, you will be lying in bed or sitting in an armchair by the window.

Whatever your circumstances, would you like to try and give yourself another kind of holiday, a time for 're-creation'. It's such a pleasant word! A little time to exist, to love, to contemplate. A little time to listen to another voice, the one near you which has so often shouted, or whispered, 'You're not listening to me!'

A little time longer, perhaps to listen to this God who speaks to us. It seems to me that today he is saying, 'Live, eat, work, fight, relax. It's necessary and it's good. But stop worrying and fretting. From time to time, stop, if only for a few minutes. Be silent. I, your God, want to speak to you: *I have something to say to you.*'

# Jesus in the Desert
# or the 'Other Aptitude'[1]

The Gospel of Jesus Christ according to
St Mark — 1:12—15

*[Jesus had just been baptised.] Immediately after-
wards the Spirit drove him out into the wilderness
and he remained there for forty days, and was tempted
by Satan. He was with the wild beasts, and the angels
looked after him.*

*After John had been arrested, Jesus went into
Galilee. There he proclaimed the Good News from
God. 'The time has come,' he said, 'and the kingdom
of God is close at hand. Repent, and believe the Good
News.'*

Jesus has a lot of work before him. He must, as
today's Gospel tells us, 'proclaim the Good News
by saying: The Kingdom of God is here! Be convert-
ed!' He hasn't a minute to lose. The entire world
has need of him. However, at first glance it would
seem that he is badly organised and wasting time.

— First, his coming on earth was not very well
timed. He should have waited for the coming of
Concorde to help him get around faster, for television through which he could address millions of
people at the same time, for computers to keep track
of all his followers, draw up profiles and compute
their needs, etc.

— Secondly, he seems to be dragging his feet.
For thirty years he remains an unknown, a simple
workman like any other, doing absolutely nothing to

1. Homily for the first Sunday of Lent.

make any sort of impact. When he finally decides to speak up and take action, he hesitates over what methods to use. He is 'tempted' to choose purely human methods, those of might and power. So he retreats and prays to his Father in long periods of silence. The Evangelists tell us, symbolically, of his forty days in the desert.

What a lot of lost time! It's very puzzling. But perhaps we don't understand his way of reasoning. Perhaps there is another method of getting things done that we don't know of, that differs from the business methods we know so well.

This is what I want us to try and understand today, by reflecting on a few aspects of this 'other apti-tude', that of prayer.

*What is the use of prayer?*

Who among you has not at one time or another said or thought: 'What good is praying? What does it offer us?' To begin with, the question is wrongly phrased. It implies that prayer is reduced to the level of a small business deal: to try and obtain as much as possible from God, for ourselves and others. This is to reason like a businessman who seeks to increase the number of his contacts and cover his needs as far as possible.

'I know many people in high places, I can always get the help I need.' And if I can include God in my list, then I may be at rest. He will help me pass my exams, find a job if I'm out of work, make me well if I'm ill. When I'm nominated, he will see that I win the election, he'll bring peace where there is war, and so on. I trust him, I put myself entirely in his hands.

Such a deformation of prayer leads to grave con-

35

sequences. It has a paralysing effect and, in extreme cases, can become a drug.

If, in a general way, our relationship with God is built on such a basis, it is distorted right from the start, just like a declaration of love which begins with 'What are you going to give me?' and where the intensity of the words 'I love you' would be in proportion to what we have got out of it. In this case, there is no love for another, but only love of self — i.e. I love myself so much that I do my best to use you and get what I can out of you.

*Praying is first of all 'being there', freely, for God*

Praying is the opposite to what I have just described. From the start, it demands nothing. But, it must be admitted, we are used to 'wanting', 'possessing'; we are increasingly prisoners, alienated by a society which is entirely organised on profit so that we become daily more incapable not only of living but of understanding the meaning of giving and thus of authentic love. Let me give you an example.

Ladies, I'm sure you've all experienced this: some night at home while you are washing up, doing the ironing, or whatever, your husband says to you, 'Leave that till later and come and sit down.' You hesitate — you've so much to do. And in any case you know that a few minutes after you sit down, he'll pick up the paper and start reading or turn on the TV, seeming quite indifferent to your presence. So then you dig your heels in: 'I'm up to my ears in work and I'm wasting my time.'

But you won't waste your time, you know. Because if working for your children, your husband, your friends, is a measure of your love for them, there is also another way of loving. Not by 'doing' something

36

for someone but by just being there, voluntarily. This is the most precious thing you can offer — your time, a little of yourself, that infinite richness of a few moments of total presence.

It is primarily at this level that prayer operates: recollecting yourself in the full sense of the word — that is, taking your whole life in your hands, the life of your body, your heart, your spirit, and offering it completely, freely and gratuitously to God; being there for him.

Then, and only then, will you be on the way to understanding the true power of prayer, one that transforms you and strengthens you for action.

## Prayer transforms us

Permit me another comparison. I live by the sea. In the summer, the beach is crowded with people. I often ask the younger ones whose great preoccupation is to get a tan, 'How do you do it? You lie there on the sand nearly naked exposing your body to the rays of the sun. You daren't move because if you do you won't tan as fast, but you feel that nothing is happening. But when you take off your bikini, you can see that you have in fact tanned!' Well, prayer and especially meditation are very much like that; to be capable of stopping even for just a few moments, stripped of all that is artificial in us, our 'clothes', our disguises, and to present ourselves naked and immobile before God to bask in the sun of his love. Here too we might feel that nothing is happening, that we're wasting time, but time given to loving and being loved is never wasted because love is life-giving.

In prayer, God gives us his life.

Some time ago I was having a conversation with a

young man whose life had not been exemplary, to put it mildly. However, he had met a girl whom he truly loved. Astonished to see him so changed, so different, I asked him, 'What has that girl done to you?' 'Nothing,' he replied, 'She *loves me!*' When love reaches us, it transforms us. When God's love touches us, it liberates and recreates us.

My friends, you can't get a tan without exposing yourselves to the sun. Similarly, you can't truly be renewed without exposing yourselves to God's infinite love.

### Prayer strengthens us for action

There are two kinds of energy in the world capable of multiplying man's forces a hundredfold by animating all his actions and his struggles. On the one hand, we have interest, ambition, pride and envy which are manifestations of self-love; and on the other, love of others, which is, consciously or not, love of God.

But selfish love of self focuses our attention on ourselves to the detriment of others and is totally destructive. Only true love, reinforced by individual and collective service to others, builds up the individual and the world.

To pray is to welcome in ourselves the energy called Love, or 'grace' as theologians call it.

To pray (whatever the form of the prayer) is to quench our thirst at the source of Love: God. 'God *IS* love' St John tells us. And this love unites us deeply, converts us, makes us turn away from ourselves and towards others; it inspires us to take up the struggle for a better world. For what distinguishes the Christian is not the choice between fighting and refusing to fight (that's a false problem), but love as a basis, a lever against egoism in ourselves, in others, and in all structures of society.

*Prayer does not demobilise man; it sends him into battle*

My friends, let us not, above all, reason like pagans. We must not suppose that prayer will magically solve all our problems; that as soon as we call on God, he will miraculously remove all obstacles from our path like a father saying to his child, 'Leave it, my child, you'll get too tired. Daddy will finish your work for you.' In that case we would have an appallingly paternalistic God who would only kill our manhood. He wouldn't respect us and therefore wouldn't love us.

Prayer doesn't preclude effort. It puts us in a state of grace, awaiting God's action. It returns us to life, but much stronger because our weaknesses have been united with God's strength. The obstacles remain and, except in rare cases, do not change. It is we, through the grace of God, who change, take up our human battles again and win.

Jesus Christ didn't waste his time in the desert while praying to his Father. He gave himself time for love to grow in him. And it's thanks to that love that he saved the world.

As for us, in this topsy-turvy life which pulls at us from all sides, in the midst of false aptitudes and false successes, are we capable of letting ourselves be 'led into the desert'? Do we know how to be silent for a few minutes in the day, while waiting for a bus or waiting for the traffic lights to change from red to green; a few minutes in the evening after turning off the TV or in the morning on the way to work.

Are we able to recollect ourselves, placing ourselves in God's axis to receive his love?

If not, we will just keep falling off balance.

But if the answer is yes, we will discover another aptitude — that prodigious aptitude called true prayer.

# The Transfiguration or the 'Other Face'[1]

The Gospel of Jesus Christ according to
St Mark — 9:2—10

*Six days later, Jesus took with him Peter and James
and John and led them up a high mountain where
they could be alone by themselves. There in their
presence he was transfigured: his clothes became
dazzlingly white, whiter than any earthly bleacher
could make them. Elijah appeared to them with
Moses; and they were talking with Jesus. Then Peter
spoke to Jesus: 'Rabbi,' he said 'it is wonderful for
us to be here; so let us make three tents, one for you,
one for Moses and one for Elijah.' He did not know
what to say; they were so frightened. And a cloud
came, covering them in shadow; and there came a
voice from the cloud, 'This is my Son, the Beloved.
Listen to him.' Then suddenly, when they looked
round, they saw no one with them any more but only
Jesus.*

*As they came down from the mountain he warned
them to tell no one what they had seen, until after
the Son of Man had risen from the dead. They ob-
served the warning faithfully, though among themselves they discussed what 'rising from the dead'
could mean.*

My dear friends, there are many who regret not
having known Jesus the way they know their friends

1. Homily for the Second Sunday in Lent.

41

today. If only they could have lived with him, how easy it would have been to love him and follow him . . . or so they think. In fact, it is an illusion. The Gospel today reveals that only long months after the apostles had joined Jesus did they discover his true identity.

It was on the Mountain — that high place where God, in biblical tradition, reveals himself — that Jesus showed his true face to his apostles, but most of all that's where he opened their eyes. Beyond the clothes and the flesh, they 'saw' the invisible; beyond the silence they 'heard' the inaudible: 'This is my beloved Son.'

But it was only momentary.

When the light in their hearts went out, the apostles saw only a man's face, heard only a man's words. They had to continue living by their faith alone just as we do today. They saw Jesus' face tired after long journeys, discouraged by the incomprehension of his people, sweating from anguish to agony, covered in blood and spittle, distorted by pain, and finally, a face frozen by death.

Beyond all those faces they had to find the face of the Son of God. They never completely found it, or recognised it. But later, the Holy Ghost was to cure them of their partial blindness.

And we, would we have recognised him? But it's not our problem, we say. Jesus of Nazareth is no longer physically among us. On the other hand, countless people are all around us. We look at them, they look at us . . . and we don't see their 'true faces' because we're disguised, we wear masks. We don't see their 'other face' beyond the flesh, the one that only a look of faith can reveal: their Son-of-God face. Because since God in Jesus Christ took the face of a man, man in Jesus Christ has taken the face of God.

O man, where is your face!

*Man's masks and his 'real face'*

My friends, who among you has not experienced the discovery or re-discovery of a person near you? When one day you exclaim (whether disappointed or thrilled), 'I've finally seen his true face!' And sometimes, you might add, 'He was so different — fairly *transfigured!*'

Few men reveal their natural face; few men display the face of their soul. Why are we so many to hide from ourselves and from everyone else? Why so many disguises and deceiving masks? Secret men who never reveal their identity. Paralysed men who are afraid of themselves. Hearts are buried, lives are repressed, only jerkily expressing themselves now and then through boasts, aggression or biting irony.

And why are we so quick to put masks on other people's faces? 'That man looks shifty,' 'That woman is really evil,' 'That boy will never come to any good,' we say. The mask of the liar, the mask of the wicked, the mask of the lazy . . . All these masks of the human carnival imprison people in *roles* and prevent them from becoming the *persons* they should be.

Why does society with its powers of information, education, propaganda, publicity and more, impose our behaviour on us? We are constantly told: 'If you want to think well, look well, vote well, if you want to be happy in your home, succeed in your business, have clean breath, silky hair, a slim waist, a whiter wash . . . buy this, eat that, listen to this, vote for that . . .'

Our experts in political conscience, economy,

aesthetics and so on, have prepared all our disguises and masks right down to the final mask in the mortuary: a pine or oakwood coffin, with or without handles, small or large cross, all relative to income of course. There are dead people and there are dead people . . . low-income, middle-income, high-income, the famous and the ordinary.

Where in all this does man come in? The human man, made of flesh, blood and spirit; original man, *because we are all prototypes* not items off an assembly line and if we try to create people in this fashion, we will only deteriorate radically ourselves.

Where is man? The one whom God watches over and loves?

There are people who die without ever having been themselves. We must rediscover the true face of each person and permit him to develop and grow.

When I used to go camping with young people, very often we would light a campfire at night. The next morning the fire would have turned into a charred mass of wood in a bed of ashes. We would either observe sadly that what had been a beautiful sight the night before had turned into a sorry mess, or, more often than not, we would poke the ashes for a few embers, put on some twigs, blow and blow and relight the fire. Then I would say to these youngsters what I want to say to you today:

'Never forget that in you, and in every person, despite the charred wood and ashes, there is always an ember. That's where we must look for man because the ashes are dead but the ember is alive. This ember in man is *real life* which springs anew every day under the breath of the Spirit and "God saw that this was good". From this life and only from it, the real face of every person will emerge.'

*The 'other face'*

The Christian must go further, much further, 'beyond' the true face of man, when his masks are snatched away from him.

St Paul said in the beginning of the Epistle to the Ephesians that God had always wanted man to be his son in Jesus Christ — that is, man has always been foremost in God's thoughts, not just a mere man but one destined to divinity. This long and prodigious 'transfiguration', the rebirth of man which is spared the 'disfiguration' of sin, began with the coming of Christ. Our personal history with our disfigured human faces as well as universal human history, has become the way to our transfigured (that is, divinised) life and face.

This prodigious destiny of man establishes his infinite dignity and the deep reasons for his struggle for total liberation:

First, his dignity. Man is infinitely greater and more beautiful than we think. Whatever the colour of his skin, his traditions, his make-up or his behaviour, man in Jesus Christ has always been from the very beginning the sacred Son of God and thus should be revered. Whoever we are, we should kneel down before one another.

Second, since man is so great, to damage him in any way becomes a crime, the greatest of all crimes. It becomes a duty, the greatest of all duties, to fight against all that defiles him and everything that stunts his growth. This is what Christ fought for here on earth. The value of one man is the price of the blood of Christ.

From now on, when man destroys himself by shutting himself up in his pride and egoism, he is crucifying Jesus.

From now on, when other men or bad education, pressures, or socio-politico-economic structures prevent a man not only from nourishing and instructing himself but from developing all his capacities, they will be crucifying Jesus Christ because Christ, to save man, united with him totally.

## Man's 'disfiguration' or his 'transfiguration'

And so we find ourselves facing the same problem as the apostles before and after the Transfiguration. We too are disciples of the same Jesus, we too walk with him and frequently we don't recognise him. Like the apostles, we come across:

*tired faces,* the face of the man on the bus returning home from work; the face of the mother who hasn't a spare minute to herself;

*discouraged faces* like the face of the unemployed person who queues up outside the Labour Exchange, and the face of the militant person who fights alone in a sea of indifference;

*anguished faces,* like the lonely aged whose offspring live at the other end of the country and whose nearby relatives will only surface at their funeral hoping the service 'won't go on forever';

*faces agonising under torture* like the face of the political prisoner in Chile, Brazil, elsewhere . . . and the haggard face of the Soviet intellectual receiving 'treatment' in a psychiatric hospital;

*faces frozen by death,* in Angola, the Lebanon, Ireland . . .

Beyond the suffering faces of our brothers, can we recognise Jesus Christ or will our recognition depend on the Word of the Father who will announce, 'He was my beloved Son!' or the Word of the Son saying, 'That was me!'

O my God, I believe in you, you who took on a human face through Jesus Christ.

O my God, I believe in man who, in Jesus Christ, must rediscover his 'real face' and begin to don his 'Son-of-God-face'.

O my God, thanks to you, man is so great . . . if only I could see it.

# The Samaritan Woman or the 'Other Thirst'[1]

The Gospel of Jesus Christ according to
St John — 4:5—42

*On the way he came to the Samaritan town called Sychar, near the land that Jacob gave to his son Joseph. Jacob's well is there and Jesus, tired by the journey, sat straight down by the well. It was about the sixth hour. When a Samaritan woman came to draw water, Jesus said to her, 'Give me a drink.' His disciples had gone into town to buy food. The Samaritan woman said to him, 'What? You are a Jew and you ask me, a Samaritan, for a drink?' — Jews, in fact, do not associate with Samaritans. Jesus replied: 'If you only knew what God is offering and who it is that is saying to you, Give me a drink, you would have been the one to ask, and he would have given you living water.' 'You have no bucket, sir,' she answered, 'and the well is deep: how could you get this living water? Are you a greater man than our father Jacob who gave us this well and drank from it himself with his sons and his cattle?' Jesus replied: 'Whoever drinks this water will get thirsty again: the water that I shall give will turn into a spring inside him, welling up to eternal life.' 'Sir,' said the woman, 'give me some of that water, so that I may never have to come here again to draw water.'*

1. Homily for the Third Sunday in Lent. This homily was based on the 1969-70 missal in which appeared the Gospel of the Samaritan Woman. It has now been deleted. We have kept the text with the permission of the copyright holders of *Jour du Seigneur*.

he liberates man and gives him the life of Christ. He is not the proprietor of this life, merely its servant.

And so my words themselves reach you because there are people to accept them, print them and spread them.

## Humans not Angels

Some people will say that a printer is faithful — he reproduces my words exactly. But sometimes priests can deform the face and Word of God. True, but let's stop dreaming of an ideal priest, a priest with a halo and an archangel's wings. Especially as different people want different wings — wings on the right, wings on the left, wings in the middle, to say nothing of wings sprouting from the top of one's head so as to be able to ascend straight into heaven! We have no wings. We are humans. If you find us lacking in knowledge or love, instead of criticising us, help us and pray we may become better people. After all, even Jesus Christ himself begged his apostles for their prayers. And don't be afraid. Whatever the weaknesses and limitations of your priest, the face and voice of Jesus Christ will always appear in the pages of the book of your life. Because Christ gave his Church a solid guarantee. There will never be a breakdown.

## Without a priest there is no Church

But despite her attractiveness and guarantee not to break down, the Church isn't some kind of machine or silent object. The Church is the faithful assembled together. The living people of Christ, Christians and priests together, carry the responsibility for this life which we must transmit to the world. It is a fact that without communities there would be no priests;

but by the same token, there cannot be a Church without priests.

My friends, we need men who are witnesses of the freely given love Jesus Christ has for his people.

We need voices to call us; at times they may merely be feeble echoes but echoes nevertheless of this Word which was given to us by God through Jesus Christ.

We need men who offer themselves up entirely to the historical perpetuation of the roots of Christ's Church.

We need men to assemble, give rise to and create communities which we can in turn found in our schools, factories, and other different centres.

We need men who are free to give themselves to the service of life, to keep Christ's sacrifice alive, for it is the perennial source which has sprung up in the heart of the world for the salvation of man.

*Priests? Why not?*

Two thousand years ago, Jesus asked this service of some fishermen, a tax inspector and others. They left everything behind and followed him.

Today, through his Church, he continues to ask the same services of good, sound men. Why should these men not respond? Would you young people not respond? Why?

Because it's too hard? Because things are 'uncertain' in 'today's' Church? Come on, let's be serious.

Do you think the man who marries a beautiful girl today knows what his wife's face will look like in twenty years?

Do you think that today's medical student can foresee what medical needs will arise in twenty years' time?

Do you think that the person sailing around the world knows what sun and what storms await him?

*Think and reflect but don't cheat yourself*

We have the right and duty to reflect and foresee but not to use our wise reflections as a pretext for not embarking. So let the Tabarlys of today's Church embark on their voyage and if some people want to sit on the prow of their ship and grumble that things are not what they used to be, or if others complain that there is too much arguing on board about the best direction to take, then let them turn away and hoist up their sails!

Where will the wind take them? I don't know. I'm not the wind. It's the Spirit which the Scriptures tell us blows where it wills. What I do know and what I believe with all my heart is that if they don't desert the ship, if they stay on board, if we all stayed on board, we would arrive together without fail because we have Jesus Christ on board with us.